For my little animal lovers,
Annabel and Grace. -L.N.

This book may be purchased in bulk at special discounts for children's ministries, camps, fundraising,
subscription boxes, classrooms, or similar purposes. Special editions can also be created.
For details, see: SeedlingsBooks.com/bulk

Written by Lila Noffsinger
Illustrated by Lucy Shin
Cover Design by Sarah Battistelli

Typeset in Linotte

Library of Congress Control Number: 2023918788

ISBN #979-8-9870941-4-3 (hardcover)
ISBN #979-8-9870941-5-0 (paperback)
ISBN #979-8-9870941-6-7 (ebook)

First Edition February, 2024
Published in San Jose, California, USA

1 3 5 7 9 10 8 6 4 2

www.lilanoffsinger.com
www.seedlingsbooks.com

Instagram: @SeedlingsBooks

A Little Christian's ANIMALS

Lila Noffsinger

Illustrated by Lucy Shin

The **snake** in
the garden told
lots of lies.

Genesis 3:1

The **dove** with the
branch proved that
land was dry.

Genesis 8:11

The **camel** brought Rebekah
to her new spouse.
Genesis 24:61

The **frogs** hopped into each Egyptian's house.

The **sheep** remind us that God knows what's best.

The **lions** in the den put Daniel's faith to the test.

The **whale** swallowed Jonah after he tried to hide.

The birds of the air showed God always provides.

Matthew 21:7-9

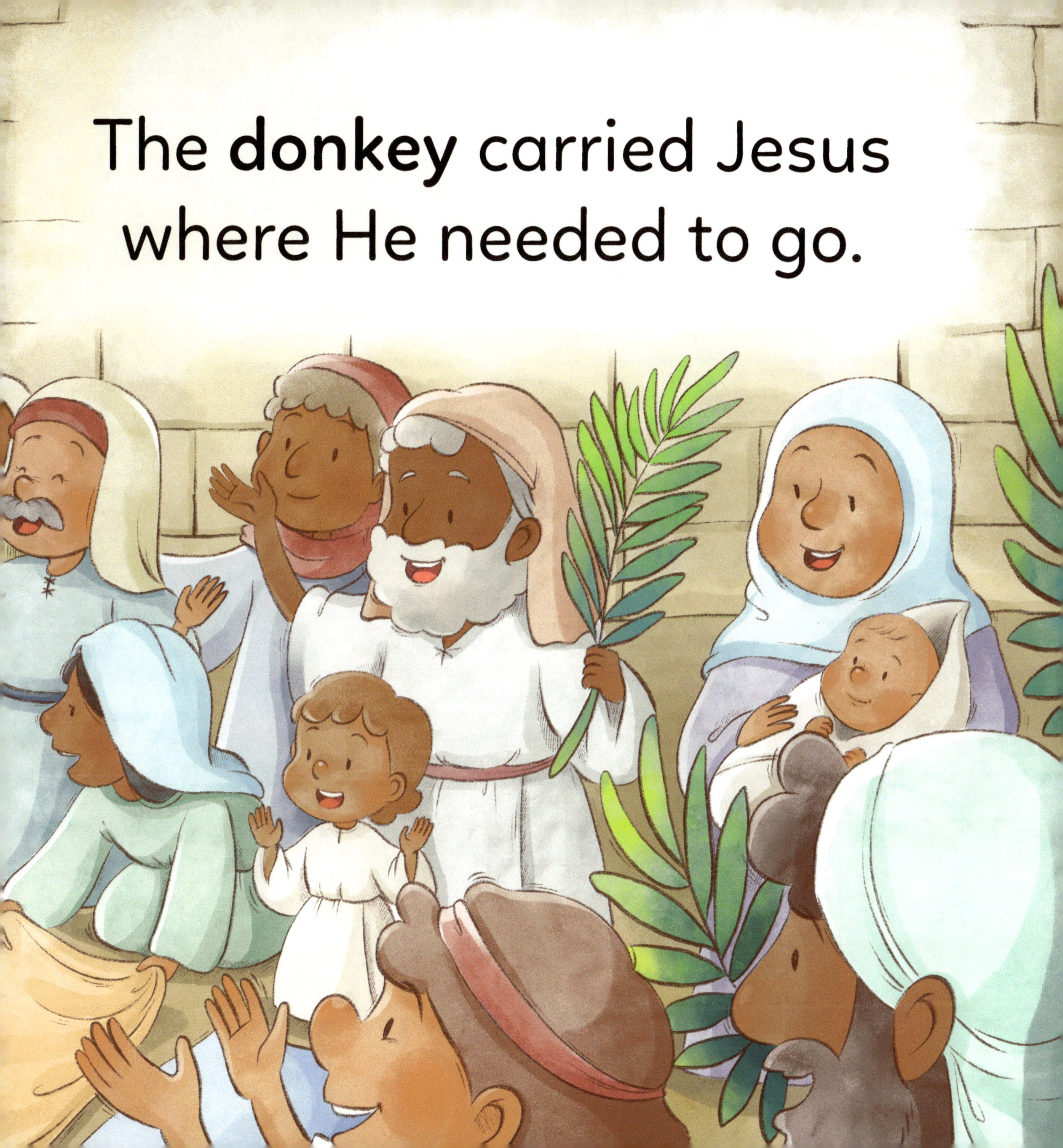
The **donkey** carried Jesus where He needed to go.

The **rooster** crowed
after Peter said no.

God made *all* animals,
weak *and* strong. . .

Isaiah 11:6-9

And when the world is new, they'll all get along!

Let's Read More. . .

Snake: Adam and Eve in Eden
Genesis 3
The Jesus Storybook Bible, 28
The Beginner's Bible, 18

Dove: Noah and the Flood
Genesis 6-9
The Jesus Storybook Bible, 38
The Beginner's Bible, 26

Camel: Isaac and Rebekah
Genesis 24
The Beginner's Bible, 52

Frogs: The Plagues in Egypt
Exodus 7-11
The Jesus Storybook Bible, 84
The Beginner's Bible, 104

Sheep: The Lord is My Shepherd
Psalm 23
The Jesus Storybook Bible, 130
The Beginner's Bible, 190

Lions: Daniel and the Lions' Den
Daniel 6
The Jesus Storybook Bible, 152
The Beginner's Bible, 251

In YOUR Bible!

Whale: Jonah and the Whale
Jonah 1-3
The Jesus Storybook Bible, 160
The Beginner's Bible, 257

Birds: Sermon on the Mount
Matthew 5-7
The Jesus Storybook Bible, 228
The Beginner's Bible, 319

Donkey: The Triumphal Entry
Matthew 21:1-11, Mark 11:1-11, John 12:12-19
The Beginner's Bible, 427

Rooster: Peter Denies Jesus
Matthew 26:69-75, Mark 14:66-72,
Luke 22:55-62

World Made New
Isaiah 11:6-9

About the Author

Lila Noffsinger loves sharing her Christian faith through the written word. When not writing or playing with her family, she likes to hike, craft, cook, and read. She lives with her husband and two daughters in San Jose, CA.

www.lilanoffsinger.com

About the Artist

Lucy Shin is an illustrator and concept artist who enjoys focusing on character design. When she is not drawing, she loves to meet up with her friends, play games, and travel with her husband. She lives with her husband in Austin, TX.

Instagram: @lucyart_s

I hope that you've enjoyed this book!
This is my heartfelt request for a review. I love creating books that kids and parents will love, but I am not very good at marketing. If you want to help other families find this book, and also help a small-time author, the BEST thing you can do is take a few seconds to leave an honest review. I read every review, and I would love to read yours.
Thank you!
-Lila
SeedlingsBooks.com/ReviewAnimals

Free Coloring Pages!

Did you know that ALL our coloring pages are available for you to **download and print for FREE!** Get access to our constantly updating library of coloring pages from *all* of our books, and start coloring today!
SeedlingsBooks.com/Color